The genuine memoirs of Dennis O'Kelly, Esq. commolny [sic] called Count O'Kelly: ...

Dennis O'Kelly

The genuine memoirs of Dennis O'Kelly, Esq. commolny [sic] called Count O'Kelly: ...
O'Kelly, Dennis
ESTCID: T040770
Reproduction from British Library
With a half-title.
London : printed for C. Stalker, 1788.
[4],72p. ; 8°

Eighteenth Century
Collections Online
Print Editions

Gale ECCO Print Editions

Relive history with *Eighteenth Century Collections Online*, now available in print for the independent historian and collector. This series includes the most significant English-language and foreign-language works printed in Great Britain during the eighteenth century, and is organized in seven different subject areas including literature and language; medicine, science, and technology; and religion and philosophy. The collection also includes thousands of important works from the Americas.

The eighteenth century has been called "The Age of Enlightenment." It was a period of rapid advance in print culture and publishing, in world exploration, and in the rapid growth of science and technology – all of which had a profound impact on the political and cultural landscape. At the end of the century the American Revolution, French Revolution and Industrial Revolution, perhaps three of the most significant events in modern history, set in motion developments that eventually dominated world political, economic, and social life.

In a groundbreaking effort, Gale initiated a revolution of its own: digitization of epic proportions to preserve these invaluable works in the largest online archive of its kind. Contributions from major world libraries constitute over 175,000 original printed works. Scanned images of the actual pages, rather than transcriptions, recreate the works ***as they first appeared.***

Now for the first time, these high-quality digital scans of original works are available via print-on-demand, making them readily accessible to libraries, students, independent scholars, and readers of all ages.

For our initial release we have created seven robust collections to form one the world's most comprehensive catalogs of 18th century works.

Initial Gale ECCO Print Editions collections include:

History and Geography
Rich in titles on English life and social history, this collection spans the world as it was known to eighteenth-century historians and explorers. Titles include a wealth of travel accounts and diaries, histories of nations from throughout the world, and maps and charts of a world that was still being discovered. Students of the War of American Independence will find fascinating accounts from the British side of conflict.

Social Science
Delve into what it was like to live during the eighteenth century by reading the first-hand accounts of everyday people, including city dwellers and farmers, businessmen and bankers, artisans and merchants, artists and their patrons, politicians and their constituents. Original texts make the American, French, and Industrial revolutions vividly contemporary.

Medicine, Science and Technology
Medical theory and practice of the 1700s developed rapidly, as is evidenced by the extensive collection, which includes descriptions of diseases, their conditions, and treatments. Books on science and technology, agriculture, military technology, natural philosophy, even cookbooks, are all contained here.

Literature and Language
Western literary study flows out of eighteenth-century works by Alexander Pope, Daniel Defoe, Henry Fielding, Frances Burney, Denis Diderot, Johann Gottfried Herder, Johann Wolfgang von Goethe, and others. Experience the birth of the modern novel, or compare the development of language using dictionaries and grammar discourses.

Religion and Philosophy
The Age of Enlightenment profoundly enriched religious and philosophical understanding and continues to influence present-day thinking. Works collected here include masterpieces by David Hume, Immanuel Kant, and Jean-Jacques Rousseau, as well as religious sermons and moral debates on the issues of the day, such as the slave trade. The Age of Reason saw conflict between Protestantism and Catholicism transformed into one between faith and logic -- a debate that continues in the twenty-first century.

Law and Reference
This collection reveals the history of English common law and Empire law in a vastly changing world of British expansion. Dominating the legal field is the *Commentaries of the Law of England* by Sir William Blackstone, which first appeared in 1765. Reference works such as almanacs and catalogues continue to educate us by revealing the day-to-day workings of society.

Fine Arts
The eighteenth-century fascination with Greek and Roman antiquity followed the systematic excavation of the ruins at Pompeii and Herculaneum in southern Italy; and after 1750 a neoclassical style dominated all artistic fields. The titles here trace developments in mostly English-language works on painting, sculpture, architecture, music, theater, and other disciplines. Instructional works on musical instruments, catalogs of art objects, comic operas, and more are also included.

biblioLife
old books. new life.

The BiblioLife Network

This project was made possible in part by the BiblioLife Network (BLN), a project aimed at addressing some of the huge challenges facing book preservationists around the world. The BLN includes libraries, library networks, archives, subject matter experts, online communities and library service providers. We believe every book ever published should be available as a high-quality print reproduction; printed on-demand anywhere in the world. This insures the ongoing accessibility of the content and helps generate sustainable revenue for the libraries and organizations that work to preserve these important materials.

The following book is in the "public domain" and represents an authentic reproduction of the text as printed by the original publisher. While we have attempted to accurately maintain the integrity of the original work, there are sometimes problems with the original work or the micro-film from which the books were digitized. This can result in minor errors in reproduction. Possible imperfections include missing and blurred pages, poor pictures, markings and other reproduction issues beyond our control. Because this work is culturally important, we have made it available as part of our commitment to protecting, preserving, and promoting the world's literature.

GUIDE TO FOLD-OUTS MAPS and OVERSIZED IMAGES

The book you are reading was digitized from microfilm captured over the past thirty to forty years. Years after the creation of the original microfilm, the book was converted to digital files and made available in an online database.

In an online database, page images do not need to conform to the size restrictions found in a printed book. When converting these images back into a printed bound book, the page sizes are standardized in ways that maintain the detail of the original. For large images, such as fold-out maps, the original page image is split into two or more pages

Guidelines used to determine how to split the page image follows:

• Some images are split vertically; large images require vertical and horizontal splits.
• For horizontal splits, the content is split left to right.
• For vertical splits, the content is split from top to bottom.
• For both vertical and horizontal splits, the image is processed from top left to bottom right.

THE GENUINE MEMOIRS
OF
Dennis O'Kelly, Esq.
COMMONLY CALLED
COUNT O'KELLY:

[Price 2s. Sewed.]

THE GENUINE MEMOIRS

OF

Dennis O'Kelly, Esq.

COMMOLNY CALLED

COUNT O'KELLY:

Containing many curious and interesting Anecdotes of that CELEBRATED CHARACTER, and his COADJUTORS on the TURF and in the FIELD, with a Variety of authentic, singular, and entertaining MILITIA MANOEUVRES, never before published.

LONDON:

Printed for C. STALKER, STATIONERS-COURT, LUDGATE-HILL.

MDCCLXXXVIII.

W. Musgrave

ERRATA.

In page 6, line 25, for *he could begin* read, *he began*.
In page 9, line 16, for *effect* read, *affect*.
In page 10, line 14, for *motion* read, *emotion*.

THE
GENUINE MEMOIRS
OF
Dennis O'Kelly, Esq.

TO perpetuate the memory, and vindicate the fame of distinguished characters, is the business and the duty of impartial Biography; but it is a business and a duty too frequently perverted and abused. The prostitution of genius, in this very depraved and excentric period, is as common and enormous as that of beauty; and the neglect, or rather contempt of truth, prevalent as that of virtue. Conscious of this literary reprobation, and viewing the consequences with abhorrence and disgust, it is the honest intention of the present Biographist, to state nothing in this narrative that will not bear the test of enquiry: and as

several

~~several spurious~~ accounts of the very extraordinary character, which is here delineated, and which, no doubt, will be succeeded by others equally delusive and erroneous,---He invites, with confidence, a comparison which must produce the verdict of authenticity.

Much controversy, and many assertions have taken place, with regard to the specific part of the sister kingdom, in which the late Lieutenant Colonel O'Kelly was born: but as that is, in our opinion, of very little consequence, we shall content ourselves in declaring that he was a genuine offspring of that nation, which has, from time to time, for more than four hundred years, produced heroes and heroins of every degree and description upon the scale of human existence.

When we say that his parents moved in a humble, perhaps a humiliating walk of life, we must, at the same time, observe with Dean Swift, "that whoever would wish to be ac-
"quainted with the true ancient nobility of
"Ireland, must resort to places of the lowest
"denomination, and converse with people of
"the very lowest classes."—A remark, which
we

we believe would hold good in every conquered country in the univerſe.

In what particular ſphere the father of our hero moved, we cannot, with certainty, advance. To be unnoted, is the privilege of obſcurity; but, his brother was ſo very low an artificer as that of a *Brogue-maker*, by which he earned a miſerable exiſtence for a numerous family. As to education, we can prove by inconteſtible evidence, that even the idea of that recommendatory and uſeful quality would never have exiſted in the family. The Colonel, before he left Ireland, was, from neceſſity, obliged to contract certain ſmall debts, for ſome of which he gave acknowledgments, ſigned only with his mark, and that ſo extremely indicative of vulgarity, that one cannot but behold him in his more elevated ſpheres, with approbation and aſtoniſhment!

Admitting, as the world muſt do, the minutiæ of his parentage, birth, and education, to be of little conſequence to our readers, we ſhall here draw a veil over the early parts of his life, and abruptly introduce him in that great, attractive variegated theatre of Europe, the metropolis of Great Britain, about the year 1748, and about the age of twenty, and, here it becomes necessary to give our readers a sketch of those qualities of mind and body, by which the gradations of his life were directed.

DENNIS KELLY, for such were his names, and by such alone could he have been distinguished in the onset, was about five feet eleven inches high, very broad in the shoulders, and equally deep chested. His legs well proportioned, and his hands finely formed by nature for those manual exertions, which nature had apparently intended them, and to which, with a laudable spirit of industry, he very shortly applied them,—*the poles of a Sedan chair*. His features were neither irregular nor unpleasing, though strongly marked with *the varnacular*; but his voice, (the very reverse of melody) not only assailed, but wounded the ear. It was what might be termed the broadest and the most offensive brogue that his nation, perhaps, ever produced. His mental attributes seemed to bear a just proportion with the stamina and

strength

strength of his body. He possessed an accurate retentive memory, and a discriminating judgment, which he had a manner of applying with advantage, and without offence, to objects which did not concern him. His intuition was not only agreeable, but surprizing, for its comprehension was universal. He had been but a short time in London before he was intimately acquainted with most characters, most events, and most probabilities. Many and oftentimes has he carried great personages, male and female, whose secret histories have been familiar to his knowledge, and often has he *blessed the honour* of those whom he well knew possessed neither that nor any other good quality. How he acquired such information, may naturally occur to discernment; but when it is known that Dennis had, by *certain recommendations*, introduced himself be-low stairs, aye, and above stairs too, into the houses of certain great folks, the wonder would be removed, at least in a great measure lessened. To those of a too sceptical disposition, the following well known fact may be fully argumentative.——One birth-day, when an unusual number of the nobility attended the annual congratulations

of

of their Sovereign, the crowd of carriages, from one end of Saint James's-street to the other, was so unusually great, that they were, in a manner, dove-tailed in each other; Dennis, and his brother *poler* Knights, plied to great advantage. A guinea was the common price of a Sedan, from the top of the street to the palace. Lady ―――, whose name, with deference and respect for her amiable family, we must keep sacred; having been a long time jammed in this uncomfortable way, at length ordered a chair, and it was the good fortune of our Hero to be her ladyship's foremost man. In helping her from her carriage, and dispersing the crowd of surrounding gapers, Dennis acted with such powers and magnanimity, that her ladyship conceived him to be a regeneration of Hercules or Hector, and her opinion was by no means altered when she beheld the powerful elasticity of his muscular motions on the way to the Royal residence. Dennis touched her ladyship's guinea, and bowed in return for a bewitching smile which accompanied it. The fatigues of this propitious day being over, he could begin to ruminate upon the profits, but more upon the smile, which in fact was given with

such

such energy and meaning, as to penetrate both head and heart; but what specific construction to form on the matter, he was utterly at a loss for. Had he been acquainted with the delicacies and refinements of high life, he would have known better. In a little time, however, the mistery was explained. The very next evening, as he was standing near the door of White's Chocolate-house, he was accosted by an elderly woman, who asked him the way to Bolton Row, and at the same time offered him a shilling to conduct her, as she was quite a stranger in London: Dennis, who knew every place, immediately accepted the offer. They arrived at the house described, and he was asked in to drink something, the weather being extremely cold. An agreeable young woman, mistress of the house, and who had been formerly chamber-maid at a noted Inn in Hounslow, opened the door, and received *the stranger in town* with great cordiality and friendship.--" Do *you* know, said she,
" addressing herself to our Hero, of any Chair-
" man who wants a good place?"   " Yes,
" Madam," answered Dennis, " 'an that I
" do: I should be very glad to be after re-
" commending myself, because I know my-
" self,

" felf, and love myfelf better than any one
" elfe."—" Why then, if you will go to
" Lady ―――, in Hanover Square, to-
" morrow morning, I think you will be
" hired; you need mention no name, but
" fay you heard of the place accidentally."—
" God in Heaven blefs you," replied Dennis,
who, toffing off his bumper of ftout brandy,
retired. The next morning our Hero dreffed
himfelf to the beft advantage, and repaired to
Hanover Square, where, after making proper
enquiries, and being introduced to the houfe
fteward, he was hired at the rate of thirty
pounds a year. A new livery was immediately ordered him, and the day following he
was to enter into actual fervice.

LET our readers but recollect, for a moment, the fenfations which our Hero experienced, when he received that fmile of complacency which accompanied Lady ―――'s
guinea, at Saint James's; and let them compare thofe fenfations with what he now felt
when waiting in the Hall for the coming
down of his new miftrefs; he perceived,
upon the landing place, the fame identical perfon, who had fo pleafed, and fo puzzel-
ed

ed his imagination: all was yet confidered as merely accidental, or rather indeed, there was no time for reflexion; her ladyfhip paffing him without the left apparent notice, hurried into the chair, and defired to be fet down at the Opera Houfe. Dennis, as foremoft man, had a fecond opportunity of obferving her ladyfhip, who, ftrange to relate! upon getting out, gave him a fecond, and more fignificant glance than when firft he faw her. Upon her return, a third affault was more formidable than either of the former, and to this was added, a purfe containing five guineas, with a fqueeze of the hand, which had, altogether, fo powerful an effect upon our Hero, as to effect that bodily ftrength fo neceffary to his duty. Upon trembling limbs, however, he performed his office, and affifted in conveying his enamoured miftrefs to her auguft manfion. The next day our Hero was kept conftantly employed in meffages to Mantua-makers, Milleners, Perfumers, Hair-dreffers, &c. and, among others, he was ordered to deliver a fmall parcel in *Bolton Row*, the identical houfe from whence he received his recommendation, and to wait until he received an anfwer; there he was

shewn

shewn into a back parlour, warmed by a prodigious fire, and lighted with four wax candles. To divert *the tedious time*, a tankard of mulled wine was presented him, and the female, from whom he received it, informed him, that her mistress was not expected home for some time: she had, however, ordered her to take *care of him,* and she was very happy in his company; she was, she said, much alarmed at being *alone*. Dennis, who never missed an opportunity of kissing a pretty girl, and improving upon female condescensions, and in whom, the warm room and hot wine began to work with extraordinary motion, replied, that "upon his soul he was equally happy, and wished to be more so,"—at the same moment raising up her *modest* down cast countenance,—who, in the name of wonder and delight did he behold, but L——— herself! As this publication is intended for the virtuous, as well as vicious eye, we must conceal from the one, what the experience of the other may easily supply. Some hours were spent in mutual happiness, and the *fair disguised*, after resuming her proper attire, departed as she came, in a Hackney-coach, which was in waiting a few doors from the house. If any
thing

thing could add to the astonishment, as well as transport of, our Hero, it was, his being detained for some time after the departure of his noble paramour. He, at first, supposed caution to be the motive, but he was soon undeceived; in a few minutes after her ladyship's departure, *the stranger in town*, who he had conducted from Saint James's-street, entered the apartment, and with infinite ease, congratulated him upon his good fortune, which she observed, would never have been complete, but for her assistance. She had, she said, taken uncommon pains to *fix* him, and she expected he would reward her in proportion. His fortune, she said, was made, and her's, as well as her mistress's, depended, in a great measure, by making their advantage of such matters. She knew, she said, that her ladyship had given him a purse, and she expected he would share it, like a man of honour. Dennis, who now began to know the value of money, hesitated for some time, and then recollecting himself, assured her with an oath, swore that he had not received a *single* guinea.—" Come, my " dear *creter*," said *the stranger in town,* " come along with me, and I'll show you the difference;" taking him by the hand, she led him to the front parlour, where, removing a small looking glass, she pointed to an aperture, from whence the disconcerted Dennis could distinctly see every part of the room, in which he and her ladyship had so long continued, as they thought, unnoticed. With reluctance and confusion, he now produced the purse, which he had not before examined, and found it contained no less a sum than twenty-five bright guineas, ten of which, the *stranger in town* claimed, as her moderate right, which she assured him she must account for to her mistress. For several months did the amorous Countess and her Hibernian Hercules carry on this illicit intercourse, and if it had not been for a discovery made by Lord ———, of a similar affair in high life, Dennis would have saved a considerable sum of money. But the consequence of this discovery was, her ladyship was turned out of doors, and all her suit dismissed, and afterwards divorced according to law.

THE money which our hero had saved in the service of this *virtuous matron*, gave him, however, a taste for ease. He could no longer endure the cold walkings and fatigues of his original
pro-

profession. He threw off the long coat, and, purchasing smart clothes, resorted to smart places, Vauxhall, the Play-house, Tennis Court, Billiard Tables, &c. &c. and there it was that he first acquired that invincible disposition for play, which proved in the end, the happy source of his good fortune, but before he obtained that knowledge, which produces *certainty*, he found himself quite run out. In vain, he applied to the generosity of those, who he then found, had plundered him; in vain he remonstrated to their feelings. But in their breasts, the seeds of humanity was corrupted, and custom had, in them, entirely obliterated all sense of shame. *Mr. Kelly*, for so he was now called, being thus reduced, became still further humbled. He was compelled to become, first, a marker at a Billiard Table; and then, to accept the same offer in a Tennis Court, where he acted as the drudge and attendant of those very persons, who had actually robbed him. In those situations, it was, that he first conversed with the great. The present Duke of Richmond, when a youth; the late Sir William Draper, of amiable and lamented memory; and several

veral who permitted, or rather obliged him, for their amusement and convenience, sometimes to take a part in their matches. His disposition for dress and play continuing, and his occasions far exceeding his means, our Hero got considerably in debt, and his creditors growing impatient, apprehensive, and angry at certain dishonourable efforts, he was at length arrested, and thrown, without money or means, into the Fleet prison. In this gloomy common wealth! this source of riches to the affluent! this accumulation of misery to the distressed! what expedient was left for human industry? While his cloaths, and a few little moveables remained, he barely existed; and when all was completely exhausted, he became, O lamentable versatility of fortune, attendant in the Tap, and lived by carrying out porter to his fellow prisoners! In this situation, he was diligent, affable, and obliging. In the tap-room, he was distinguished for his jolly song, and his reputation extending to the private apartments, his company was frequently solicited among convivial circles. That well known priestess of the Cyprian Deity, that love and mirth admiring votress, to pleasing sensuality, the well

known

known Charlotte Hayes, was then an inhabitant of the same mansion, when, under all the real horrors of imprisonment, she did not forget to perform her midnight orgies, or sacrafice to the powers of love and wine. The same attributes which attracted the notice of Lady ———— soon caught the well experienced optics of Charlotte, and the same services as soon obtained, though in an infinitely less degree, the same kind renumerations. Mr. Kelly, quitting the meneal avocation of tapster, now devoted the whole of his time to Charlotte, and Charlotte, in return, devoted to him, not only her person, but her purse: time passed without care, and attachment became so strong, that no circumstance in future life, could ever dissolve or shake the union. Charlotte had many friends, it is true, but policy induced her to see them with complaicency. Her affections were still centered in our Hero, and on him were all the pecuniary favours, which she received from others, bestowed with unbounded liberality. Hence, after a durance of three years, he was enabled to liquidate his debts, and once more to immerge from the restrictions of a prison! and with him the fair source and partner of his liberty. We
must

must not, though it had almost slipped our memory, forget to mention a circumstance which occurred to our Hero whilst he remained in the Fleet prison, and which, though apparently trifling to the unambitious, facilitated the fame and fortune, which he afterwards acquired. There are, in this varied world, certain aspiring geniuses, who purchase titles, even at the expence of reputation; such as Generals without command or commissions, and Knights, whose ribbands alone bear the blush of modesty. There are others, who extort, or are not ashamed to accept of titles from the Majesty, whose power and consequence they have abridged; and there are others also, who with the genuine spirit of true nobility, let their actions claim what their high sense of honour disdains to challenge! Of this latter sort, was the Hero of these Memoirs. We have already observed, in just compliment to his taste, that he was fond of displaying his person, in point of dress, to the best advantage. Hence it was, that wherever fortune favoured him with pecuniary donations, his wardrobe was, literally speaking, exceedingly splendid! A gentleman, who had been for some time an inhabi-

tant

tant of the Fleet, became at length so very popular, as to produce a revolution in government. From democratic, he had the address to establish a monarchical constitution, and, like King Theodore, was unanimously elected Sovereign, by the full suffrage of the people: by the bye, like Theodore, he died a victim to inhumanity, and a disgrace to Great Britain. This potentate, observing our Hero's bias, bestowed upon him the title of *Count*, which spontaneous and voluntary honour he retained to the last moments of his existence, with unquestionable and universal approbation.

IN a short time after the emancipation from the Fleet, he became intimately acquainted with a class of beings commonly known by the denomination of black legs, that is, those Equestrian Heroes, who are invariably seen at every capital Horse-race in England; among those, he acquired an irresistible taste for the same avocation. He was soon initiated, and as soon became an adept in the profession. The famous horse, Eclipse, bred by the late Duke of Cumberland, was, that time, to be disposed of, and
the

the Count hearing that a friend had interest and inclination to purchase a share, prevailed upon him to let him in for a part thereof; the bargain was accordingly made, and the Count's interest, in the first instance, amounted to half a leg, that is, the one half of a quarter. The prodigious successes of Eclipse, are too well known to need observation in this place. He kept the turf for many years, and long before the meridian of his fame; the Count, growing œconomical, saved money enough to purchase out the other proprietors, and to become sole owner of the best, and most fortunate horse, both as to speed and breed, in the world; But the great advantages of the first, were soon lost by the intoxication of his master, who being too much elated with good fortune, gave a challenge, by which, though he succeeded in the instance, he defeated all future expectations. The case was this. A set of established *knowing ones*, with whom the Count was spending a convivial evening, began to depreciate the merits of Eclipse, and alleged, that his successes depended more upon chance, and the imperfections of those horses, who ran against him, than his own abilities.

The

The bait took, and the Count instantly offered any wager, that Eclipse should distance one or two horses then mentioned. A day was accordingly appointed, and such was the wonderful swiftness of Eclipse, that he won with ease. The Count, however, shortly found himself taken in, for the consequence was, that no horse in England would enter the list of competition with Eclipse after. The count, notwithstanding found consolation in the prodigious emoluments which he derived from him as a stallion, and his numerous progeny, have, for the most part, inherited all the qualities of their ancestors.

About this time, his favourite and patroness, Charlotte, took a very elegant house in King's place, and the Count, whose affections were unaltered, assisted in the double capacity of lover, and, to use a phrase of a late coinage, a flash-man, which was nothing more than a generous protector from the violence of modern buckism.

And now we come to treat of our Hero, in a situation, which, to those who know the

form

form of a Militia Commission, that "his Ma-
"jesty reposing special trust and confidence in
"the *loyalty, courage,* and *conduct*" of the hol-
der, will appear extraordinary indeed, and which
we are called upon to account for, by the following narrative. About the year 1760,
when the militia was first settled upon its
present establishment, the county of Middlesex, to its disgrace, was extremely backward
in raising their proportion of national defence. The city of Westminster had not
taken a single step towards a measure so
necessary and patriotic, at a time when the
regiments of other counties were fit for actual service. A well known military, turbulent
Scot, whose family had been active in the
Rebellion of 1745, and had suffered much in
the Stewart cause, conceiving this to be a
good opportunity of filling his pocket, and
retrieving his lost honours, set about raising a
regiment in Westminster and with such activity
and zeal did this bold bustling North Britain
proceed in the business, that Government
noticed his exertions, and promised to establish
the regiment so soon as three-fourths of the
commissions should be filled up. This was,
however, a more arduous and difficult matter;
than

than was at first conceived. The *military mania*, did not, at that time rage, as was the case during the last war, and many of the more respectable corps remaining unofficered; what must be the supposed situation of this band of illustrious City Mermidons! The indefatigable energy, however, with which the undaunted Scot proceeded, was not to be repelled. He ransacked the town and its vicinities, and, holding out commissions indiscriminately;-------- among the motley group, our Hero stood conspicuous, as an Ensign, from which station he rose, by regular gradations, and with a regular good character, to the rank of Lieutenant Colonel.

THE compliment of commissions, being at length filled up, Mac Gregor, for such was the name of the Caladonian adventurer, attained his point. It was called the Westminster Regiment of Middlesex Militia, and Mac Gregor was appointed Adjutant, the only lucrative situation in the corps. In a short time after he contrived to be appointed Captain, and was, in fact, every thing in the regiment, from Serjeant to Colonel. Commissions

missions and halberts were sold, like any other marketable commodities; and, strange and unprecedented as it may appear, every promotion depended upon a *douceur* to Mac Gregor! For instance; a *certain taylor*, and well he may be called *certain*, being so, both by name and profession, had some knowledge of the Adjutant, and actually bought a company for about two hundred pounds, which was then considered to be a prodigious price. However, Snip, like his namesake in the pantomime, was determined to repel the foe, and, therefore, borrowing the money from a friend, he quit his sheers and his shop-board, and, like a bold warrior, entered the lists of martial enterprize. We must, indeed, confess, that in this, like honest Joe, he was stimulated by his wife, whose ambition to be a Captain's lady, forced her obliging husband into all the dangers of a campaign, and compelled him to return home with the head of a conquered flea, instead of a Swiss guard's, upon the point of his polished needle; after such a glimpse as this character and appointment must give our Readers, they will naturally wonder, that a man of title, rank, fortune, and character, could be prevailed upon to take any command

mand in the Westminster division of Middlesex Militia; yet, wonderful to relate, Sir Thomas Frederick, a gentleman, possessing all those claims, was bold enough, in a moment of seduction and conviviality to take the command; and no less a respectable character, than Sir John Gibbons, inveigled, by a precedent so distinguished, accepted the Lieutenant Colonelcy. The difference of situation between those gentlemen and the other officers, was truly remarkable and ludicrous. Lamb, the Major, (not the Lamb immortalized by Foote) was a common mechanic, we believe, a watch-maker; and the Captains and Subalterns were, in general, really so low and obscure, as to be beneath the level of contempt or observation.

From this period, until the late war, when the militia was called into actual service, in the Spring of 1778: we must quit the Count's military character, and speak of him in the more interesting and more professional avocation of a gambler, whose whole time was, without interruption, devoted to play and chance. The *manœuvre* which prevented ed him from running Eclipse, reduced, or at least restricted him very much in his circumstances. The breed of that distinguished animal, were yet too young for service, and, tho' the highest expectations were formed of their success, it was with the utmost difficulty, the Count could support the expence of keeping and training them, they were, literally speaking, at times, upon *short allowance*. In the years 1775, 1776, and 1777, to such shifts was he driven, that temporary sums were raised upon part of his moveable property. Charlotte began to grow close fisted; she had been drained for many a long day, and being but a shallow mistress of speculation, thought the old proverb, of the bird in hand, the best guide of her conduct: she therefore saved her money, and with such savings, built the house on Clay-hill, near Epsom, which, upon retiring from business, she lived in, with great elegance and hospitality, and of which, the Count was ostensible master. The furniture was of the first class, and the ornaments, which by the bye, had been, it is said, from time to time, presented for meretricious services done in King's Place, were various and magnificent.

THE

The dispositions of Charlotte and the Count, were in most respects congenial, but in nothing did they more entirely vibrate, than in hospitality and good living. They kept open house during the time of every public meeting; and the Count possessing, among other happy talents, that of reconciling apparent opposites, contrived to entertain the Peer and the Black Leg at the same table. The Duke of Cumberland and Dick England; the Prince of Wales and Jack Tetherington; Lord Egremont and Ned Bishop; Lord Grosvenor and Monsieur Champreaux; the Duke of Orleans and Jack Stacie; Messieurs Leech, Piggot, Davis, Twycross, &c. &c. &c. &c. were frequently seen at the same table, and circulating the same bottle with equal familiarity and merriment. It must, however, be remarked, to the honour of the host, that he never, on any account or pretence whatsoever, permitted play, or betts of any kind, to be made at his table, or in his house; nor would he ever propose or accept the most trifling wager in private company; for whenever an attempt of that kind was made, he immediately, and with decision, asserted the prerogative of his Castle,

Castle, and extinguished the purpose in the very moment of its first glimmering.

Such were the hospitalities, such the good living, and such the conduct of Clay-hill. Who keeps the best house in England? was the frequent question.—O! Kelly, by much—Who the best wines? O! Kelly, by many degrees.—Who the best horses? O! Kelly's beat the world.—Who the pleasantest fellow? who? O! Kelly.—In short, such was the frequent use of that ejaculatory vowel upon every occasion, referring to the Count, that at length it became incorporated with his original name, and the harsh gutteral of the consonant K, was softened by the modest melody of the liquid O.—No more humble Dennis Kelly.—No more Mr. Kelly.—No more Count Kelly! we must, in future, at least until his military promotion adds consequence to his prior additions, call him by no less a title than Count O'Kelly; who, claiming the genealogy of Irish potentates, from the days of the Spanish emigrant, Mellisus, declared himself equal in point of nativity, to the greatest men in Europe.

As

As soon as the restrictions above mentioned, were intirely removed by the auriferous atchievements of the prolific Eclipse, the Count's mind, which was restricted in proportion, began to expand to a degree of liberality, and indeed munificence, rarely met with among the children of chance. He was attentive to the distresses of his friends, and, with a generous hand, relieved the indigent. It was his pride to contribute to public and private charity, without distinction of country or religion; and his relations, who were, for the most part, acquainted with poverty alone, he visited with bounty and affection.

His brother, who lived in Ireland, and was, as above hinted, a disciple of the famous Prince Crispin, he sent for, and, if his natural talents had admitted of improvement, or could have been applied to a more respectable avocation than superintendant, or what is jocularly called Master of Horse to the Clay-hill stables, Philip would have certainly moved in a more exalted sphere; but his ability, as well as ambition, being gratified, he went through the duties of that humble station,

with

with chearfulnefs and unabated affiduity; the latter of which was the leading feature in him as well as his elder brother.

He alfo invited his two nieces and their mother to participate his good fortune, and placed them in eligible fituations, and his nephew, the gentleman who fucceeds to his poffeffions, he fent abroad, in the handfomeft and moft gentleman like manner, to finifh an education, which originated in Ireland, at his uncle's fole expence.

Having made thofe feveral domeftic and family arrangements, O'Kelly devoted the whole of his time, except when called to the annual meeting of his regiment, to his ftud, and to the fpeculations of the turf, in which he difcovered fuch ftrong and fcientific abilities, as aftonifhed his coadjutors, and puzzled, and confounded his competitors; and, in the practice of which, he was feldom unfortunate. So accurate were his calculations, that happy was the man who could obtain, even a fincere *hint* of his motives; but his fecrets were in general, indeed, almoft invariably confined to his own breaft. He has been

been accused, and we believe with some truth, of deceiving those, to whom he professed attachments; and a certain *French Editor*, who lost 500l. by betting, according to his advice, was once near putting an end to his existence, with a heavy poker; the blow was however warded off by the interposition of a friendly arm, and the lives of two *excentric characters* saved to the community.

Notwithstanding the prodigious influx of money, which our Hero derived from the sources already mentioned, such were the enormous expences of his stud, his house, and his donations of friendship; and, consanguinity, that in the year 1778, we find him again streightened in his circumstances, in so much, as to borrow money on his diamond ring, to assist the expences of joining the regiment, which was, in the spring of that year, embodied and ordered on actual service. We have already observed that he was an Ensign, but at this time, we find him advanced to the rank of Captain of Grenadiers. Having fortunately met with the public newspapers of that period,

period, in which the histories of the several officers of the Westminster division of Middlesex Militia, who marched towards the sea coast, to repel the then threatned invasion, are candidly developed, we must not withhold from our Readers, an exhibition, which, from the humour and singularity of its nature cannot fail of giving entertainment. Indeed it is so immediately connected with the remainder of this Memoir, that we could not, without injury, keep it back.

Mr. James Chauvel, the Colonel, had formerly been a waiter at Saint Alban's Tavern, to which he succeeded as Master. This gentleman, from what cause we cannot assert, was distinguished but for few stricking qualities, among which were those of excessive meanness, and *bashfulness*, a character the very reverse from what might be expected in a Vintner. He had also an irresistible passion of peculation*, and the wretched men, under the

mockery

---

* With such an arbitrary hand was this description of *secret martial manœuvres* carried on, that the Colonel, in conjunction with the Agent and Major, actually withheld

even

mockery of his command, suffered excessive hardships on account of his avarice.

The post of Lieutenant Colonel was filled by one Burbridge, an honest Farmer, and a man totally ignorant of military discipline, *Honest Hodge*, never failed to communicate the misapplication of the Lord Lieutenant in giving him a military command. For example, whenever he was applied to on regimental business his uniform answer was, "What do you ask me for? I do not know."

The Major, without whose knowledge and activity it is impossible for discipline to exist, was a Mr. Barlow, a superannuated

---

even a part of the Captains pay, and for which one of them, (Matthew Hamilton) at the conclusion of the War, commenced an action and recovered a Verdict to a considerable amount. The Colonel's propensity to *save* his *cloathing* was not altogether singular. Coxheath Camp was once in confusion, from the murmurs of another Militia Regiment respecting the cloathing, and it was no uncommon sight to see our provincial troops as ragged as Falstaff's. This is accounted for when the reader is informed that government issues *money* to the commanding Officers for the cloathing of Regiments, and that they consequently go *the nearest way to work*.

Mercer,

Mercer, and so complete a martyr to the gout, that one of his feet was inverted into that form by which the inveterate foe of man is distinguished; but, as a Major, disabled from walking, might yet be an active Officer on horse-back, an acquaintance with the one would have absolved him from inconveniences of the other. To the disgrace however of the Westminster corps, Barlow was equally incapable of both. Bred behind a counter, his journies on horse-back never exceeded the * *Cockney's round*, or those of Major Sturgeon, and his figure, could scarcely be exceeded by the caracature of a Bunbury.

As eldest Captain we must now introduce our Hero.— The station which he held he considered but as merely convenient to a vanity which could be by no means condemned. It not only gave him a real denomination, but the additions of a gentleman, and it was with that view, and

* Hamstead and Highgate are called " The Cockneys round" from the Plebeians flogging their hired hacks to the first, and returning through the latter village home.

no other, he condefcended to fuftain it. Upon every occafion he was feen at the head of the Grendaier Company; and it is but juftice to obferve, that he bore the moft foldierly appearance of any officer in the regiment. Of difcipline he was, at this time, totally ignorant, and whenever he attempted to perform the moft trifling evolution, he betrayed an aukwardnefs, that immediately difcovered his general deficiency. In fupport of that fuperior perfonal afpect, which he always maintained, he was conftantly attended by an expenfive retinue, carriages, &c. and Charlotte, who travelled in the rear of his company, with her feparate fuite.

The officer next in rotation, was the redoubted Gregor Mac Gregor, by whofe activity the regiment was originally raifed. From its eftablifhment to this period, he had held the poft of Adjutant. He was a pupil of the old military fchool, and as far as ancient prejudices would admit, knew what he was about; but growing unfit for the activity of his ftation, he was permitted to difpofe of it, for about one thoufand guineas, and retained as a nominal Captain in the regiment.

The third Captain was Mr. Thomas Sockwell, formerly a Tea-dealer, but who had quitted the effluvia of that effeminate calling, and, in obedience to the rougher calls of martial fame, refigned the fcoop, and affumed the fpontoon. Whatever might have been this gentleman's original character, it was impoffible, at this time, to determine; it was loft " in fecond childifhnefs, and mere oblivion."

Mr. JAMES TAYLOR, (the Taylor)—The fourth link in this extraordinary chain of Captains, we have already glanced at. He was, on account of his profeffional prejudices, fo univerfally difliked, as to be, what the army terms, *fent to Coventry*; nothing, however, could extinguifh that extraordinary heroic fpirit, which urged him to relinquifh his trade. He had *purchafed* his Commiffion, and was refolved, however odious to the regiment, to enjoy the diftinguifhed appellation of Captain. This gentleman held Court Martials and Courts of Inquiry, at total defiance. The Colonel was his friend, and he fnapt his fingers at every fubordinate enemy. This *worthy*, is, we obferve by the militia
lift,

list, in consequence of the death of O'Kelly, the first for promotion to the *majority*.

THE fifth was Mr. William Parsons, early in life, a boatswain's mate in the Navy. On the conclusion of a former war, having saved some prize money, he retired to, what in the redundant luxury of his ambition appeared both ease and happiness, a little snug Ale-house, in London or Westminster. He contrived, hovever, to agree tolerably well with the regiment, except with our Count, who held repeated arguments with him, on the score of *education*, and, who having acquired the advantage of writing his name, made that the test of superiority.

WHEN Mr. Parsons sent his qualification from the head quarters, he employed a confidential private soldier as his amanuensis, but the letter was so utterly unintelligible, that the clerk of the peace could by no means decypher it. He accordingly communicated the difficulty to Captain Parsons, who, together with his amanuensis, in the character of a servant, came up to town, for the sole purpose of explanation. For this curious anecdote we are indebted to Mr. Selby, the Northumberland factotum, who gives it at full length, with infinite ridicule and risibility.

The youngest, and the most excentric Captain in the corps, was Mr. William Hundeshagen, a native of the Netherlands, and a man, whose indigence of pocket, mind, and person, was equally evident. He was about six feet in altitude, and yet, so miserably anatomized by famine and disease, that he had not six ounces of flesh upon his whole frame. Time, also, had ungenerously thinned his locks, and scattered over his ancient cranium, the grisley blossoms of approaching dissolution. His hands and feet were of that uncommon form, which we observe in our modern *Castratos*; when nature diverted from its regular courses, wanton in the joints, and extremities of the human body: His knees were so extremely inverted, as to form an obtuse angle with his feet, and to rub the knees of his breeches into constant tatters. To these personal defects, we cannot avoid adding, that Hundeshagen was the acknowledged *toad-eater* of Sir Thomas Frederick, who, not only treated him with contempt and inhumanity, but actually invited

the

the other officers to make him the butt of their ridicule and ill-nature.

It has been already mentioned, that Mac Gregor was permitted to dispose of his Adjutancy for a thousand guineas. The person who made that purchase, now becomes the object of remark. Mr. Whitfield, for such was his name, was, by birth, a gentleman, and brought up a soldier: he had been a Captain in the army, and enjoyed the liberal donation of half-pay. Being of an active disposition, and wishing to improve his little savings, he entered the corps in the only profitable station, that of adjutant; soon, however, disgusted at the idea of subordination among a set of men, whom he secretly despised; he contrived to redispose of his Commission at an advanced price, and upon undertaking to raise an additional Company, which by the bye, the officers did not scruple to say, that he obtained his men from the Companies already established. The Colonel, thought proper to wink at the abuse, and there being then no general muster, the thing was passed over without public notice. At Plymouth, Mr. Whitfield grew weary of his

situation

situation as Captain also, and, with the concurrence of the Colonel, accepted from one Len, a considerable douceur for the succession.

BEING released from Militia duty, Mr. Whitfield was again devoted to temporary inaction, and, being possessed of indefatigable industry, and happily aided by uncommon effrontery, he offered his services to government, to raise a regiment. He was at first refused, but such was his extraordinary perseverance, that he at length overcome every objection, and brought Sir George Young to a concurrence. The war, however, being over, and the corps of course disbanded, we now find Mr. Whitfield, still intent upon public service, a magistrate for the City of Westminster, taking his rotine of *civil duty* with his worthy Coadjutors.

WE cannot dismiss this part of our narrative without observing, that when the Westminster Militia was far distant in the West of England, the several Manœuvres thereof, and therein, private, and public, were well known in the South. The volunteer company was, during

that

that period, at Twickenham, and Twickenham was the medium of all communications. The vigor of Mr. Whitfield's difpofition was not eafily fuppreffed, and it is more than probable, that his intervals of military recefs were filled up with efforts of literary information.

Having with impartial truth defcribed this moft extraordinary and heterogenious corps of officers, it would be injuftice not to contraft their deficiences and demerits with the no lefs extraordinary good conduct of the private man, who though deprived of ability in command, yet acted with a degree of fpirit that did them honour. At Plymouth, when many regiments were tormented by divifions and difobedience, the Weftminfter Militia was actually an example of regularity and alacrity, as far as fuppofition will admit, in undifciplined foldiers. At one time, when the fleets of France and Spain were feen hovering at an inconfiderable diftance from the fhore, there were innumerable defertions, and one from the Wiltfhire, who lay neareft the fea, and next to this corps. The privates of the Middlefex taking fire at fuch ignominious conduct in thofe, who before had looked on

them

them with an eye of inferiority, could scarcely be prevailed upon to restrain their resentment, and from turning the arms, intended to repel a foreign enemy, against their own dastardly countrymen. But, to illustrate still further, the striking difference between officers and soldiers, it is worthy of remark, that at Coxheath, when the former were scolding, striking, kicking, and bruising each other like Billingsgates, and porters, two of the private men, having a serious quarrel, agreed to decide the matter like gentlemen, and actually appeared in the front of the line with drawn bayonets for that purpose. The spectacle was so uncommon, and the rebuke to their commanders so bold and direct, that it became a topic of comparative conversation in all public and private circles, and rendered the *Commissioned Heroes* of the corps still more and more odious and ludicrous.

THUS officered, and thus manned, was the Middlesex Militia during its marches from London to Gosport; from Gosport to Plymouth; from Plymouth to the extremities of Cornwall; from thence to Chatham, from Chatham to Lancaster, and from Lancaster

caster to London again, were disembodied, a circuit which occupied a space of five years! Count O'Kelly, however, did not at any time, or on any occasion, sacrifice to that duty his more profitable avocations: he and his soft associate, Charlotte, were frequently on the road, travelling with magnificence, and the Count, as usual, always present at, and the life and spirit of every principal race meeting in England. The offspring of Eclipse carried all before them, and the coffers of his master again teemed with riches. The usual rotine of gaiety and friendship was continued, and Epsom, and its proximities, felt the good effects of his social and generous disposition. But though our Hero did not sacrifice to military enthusiasm, he, nevertheless, attended every important and necessary duty. When the vaunting vanity of our national enemies threatened us with an invasion, which in fact, they never intended to attempt; no man could possibly evince a braver, or a more active and determined courage. Upon every alarm he appeared all ardour, and ready to push himself into the post of honour; and as this was the criterion of true heroism among the officers, his real and animated spirit formed a

G striking

striking contrast to those higher in command. We do not mean to insinuate a *general panic* in the corps, for most of them behaved with unexceptionable resolution, but the conduct of others, particularly the Colonel, threw the whole into universal derision. The medical effects of fear are well known to individuals; so strongly did that *purgative* work upon the constitutions of some of those we allude to, that the *temple of Cloesina* became the alternate and eternal Citadel of their prowess. So conspicuous and predominant was the effect of fear upon them, that the other officers were actually deterred from obeying the dictates of nature. On the unfortunate capture of the Ardent Man of War, who mistook the combined fleets, for that of Great Britain, every broad-side which she fired upon the headmost ships, previous to her striking her colours, was answered by the most violent explosions of flatulency from this odoriferous fortress, while the soldiers were cheering upon the hopes of a general engagement between the two fleets.

It was upon this occasion, and others of a similar nature, that O'Kelly used to laugh loud

loud and inceſſantly. "Where are your "field officers now," cried the Count! "Come forth from your S——— houſes, "your Counting-houſes, and your pecu- "lating deſks! here's the enemy on the "beach!" But ſuch vociferous ſummons's had not the deſired effect. The firing having ceaſed, that moſt magnanimous of all mili- tary Heroes, Captain Taylor, at length, came forward. His manly eyes ſuffuſed in tears, and his palid viſſage, expreſſive of equal grief and horror; "My dear friend," ſaid he, "you ſee what we have brought "ourſelves to; a pretty affair this, to be "knocked o'the head by the French; I "wiſh to God you would ſtep in and ſee "me ſign my will. As you are a gentle- "man, and a man of ſenſe as well as cour- "age, I requeſt you will do me the favour "to draw it out for me, and accept the "office of executor." The Count, who at firſt, imagined this requeſt to be an inſult to his literary deficiency, was preparing to anticipate his apprehenſion, by putting him to death in reality, but the other moſt ſeriouſly and ſolemnly aſſuring him, that he meant nothing more than what he expreſſed. The rage subsided, and after sufficiently venting his resentment at such pusillanimous conduct, the Count calmly advised him, *not to make his will till* after the *danger was all over*. On the parade, at the mess, and every where did the Count, with repeated and loud risibility, relate the story of *Fort Cloefina*. The regular returns of artillery, from that quarter, and the woeful countenance of the testamentary Captain, who, when the firing was really all over, lost every idea of a will.

To such a pitch of sovereign contempt did the military conduct of those gentlemen, and certain other field Officers throw them in the opinion of Captain O'Kelly, that he convened a general meeting of the corps, and proposed that a spirited application should be made to the then Duke of Northumberland, Lord Lieutenant of the County, to have them removed; a letter was accordingly written, and, signed by more than twelve of the corps, requesting his Grace would redeem the regiment from the disgrace in which the mental and bodily infirmities of those men had involved it. At the head of those signatures

was

was Captain O'Kelly's, and next to him, that of Captain Whitfield. This address appeared in the public papers of the day; but whether from the extreme badness of the composition, or what motive we know not, it was answered by no means agreeably to the wishes of the party. In a few words his Grace desired he should hear no more of the matter!

Such, however, was the general desire of having the regiment dismembered of those obnoxious *limbs* (our readers will excuse the pun) that a second meeting took place, and a second letter, and more spirited paper was drawn up, and signed as before. Upon this occasion the debates ran to an uncommon length, so high, indeed, as to threaten the usual consequences of a Polish Diet! the Colonel's party, however violent in harrangue, were nevertheless, too feeble for the exercise of arms, and the assembly broke up in the fermentation of words alone.

This second paper (or remonstrance) being presented to the Lord Lieutenant was somewhat more graciously attended to. His advice was, however, to let the business drop,

peace

peace he observed would soon suspend Militia duty, and humanity (which he also recommended to the Officers) induced him to let the poor men retain their stations. They were, he observed, in general old; and, nature would shortly accomplish what the appellants so much, and, perhaps with so much propriety demanded.

THE several marches and counter marches of this invincible regiment, were constantly participated by Charlotte, and, whether the God of love had, during those times, presented her at the alter of Hymen, we do not presume to ascertain. Certain it is, that if reputation, and cohabitation, were sufficient evidences of Matrimony, the performance of that ceremony must have been confirmed in the minds of the World. Yet, not less certain is it, that while she, together with the Count's Nephew, then Lieutenant O'Kelly, was in the West of England, she was arrested for a considerable sum, by the name of *Charlotte Hayes*. The debt was contracted while she supported the *Cyprian Temple* in King's Place; and was rather *neglected* than *with-held*; for, it must be

acknow-

acknowledged that, during her several campaigns with the Militia, no woman could have maintained a better conduct. Her conversation was delicate and agreeable, and her manners conciliating, from gentleness and modesty. Every engagement was religiously fulfilled, and every debt honourably discharged. When this accident took place the Count was at York; but such, and so universal was the respect in which Charlotte was held; indeed such were her claims upon friendship and gratitude, that the Officers would have, not only, discharged the action, but dismissed the Bailiffs, *extempore*, perhaps, to that Country where *lattitats* are not permitted. It was, however, thought more advisable to give bail, that the true nature of the debt might be known, and the exact balance ascertained; and this was accordingly done, what became of the matter afterwards, is by no means material; it is only mentioned here as an unquestionable evidence of that esteem, which the conduct of Charlotte, at that time, so well deserved, and which she so liberally enjoyed.

WHEN this transaction took place, we have already observed the Count was at York,

He

He was attending the races; which were remarkably crowded that season. The breed of the unrivalled Eclipse, as usual, kept her field; and the Count's speculations were more than usually fortunate. He carried every thing before him! But his successes were unfortunately followed by an accident which not only destroyed all his popularity on the turf, but had nearly put a period to his life. His winnings were by no means adequate to the pecuniary consequences of a transaction which irritated and surprized the World.

In direct opposition to the fate of a celebrated and unfortunate states-man, * it was the Count's lot always to occupy *the best inns, best rooms,* and to sleep in the softest and most sumptuous bed. Having, as usual, secured an apartment, and a bed of this description, and having had three nights peaceable occupation, it could never enter his thoughts that any person, Male or Female, would attempt disturbing his possessions. However, it so happened, that on the fourth night,

---

* Villers,-Duke of Buckingham.

after

after drinking freely, and enjoying much conviviality, he took what is commonly called *French leave* of his companions, and going softly to his chamber, found the door fastened; whether locked, or but slightly bolted, we cannot positively affirm; but, it was in such a situation, as to be opened with little difficulty. An extinguished candle stood on a chair by the bed, which was closed all round, naturally excited no small degree of wonder; curiosity was incidental. The Count gently drawing back the silken curtain, to his astonishment and delight, beheld a most enchanting female countenance!

THE chissel of Bonerotto! the pencil of Corregio! never formed more captivating charms. For some time our Hero stood, like Cymon, the celebrated clown, when he first beheld the beauties of the sleeping Ephigenia; but his emotions subsiding, cautious, and almost deprived of breath, he looked round the apartment, in hopes of discovering some articles of dress, or ornament, which might lead to conjecture, who this lovely intruder was; but in vain,

H

he could only discover a fashionable riding-dress, a watch, without any particular mark of distinction, and the other common accommodations of women. After some time, he resolved to let delicacy and honour predominate; but passion, stimulated by too much champaigne, proved too powerful. He conjectured, and perhaps with probability, that this beautiful female, being enamoured of the vast sums, he was publicly known to have won at the meeting, devised that method of securing, by artifice, and agreeable surprize, what a more regular plan might have failed in effecting. No sooner did this idea start into his heated imagination, than, regardless of all restraint, he commenced such violent hostilities, as soon awoke the terrified, unknown, object of his sensuality. In an instant she started up, and screaming with extreme vociferation soon alarmed the house. In vain our Count endeavoured to parley; in vain to pacify; the chamber door was soon attacked by numbers, and he was obliged to escape, with difficulty, out of the window, which was, by accident, convenient for the purpose. The lady, who was altogether as chaste, as she was charming, proved to be

the

the daughter of a Roman Catholic Baronet in that county. She related the particulars of the accident, as well as her fright and knowledge, would permit; and her friends being numerous and powerful, would, but for her prudent and amiable entreaties, have made an instant example of her intended ravisher. The affair, however, did not end here, a prosecution ensued, and the matter would have been brought into a Court of Law, had not the Court, by the interposition of *certain great men*, contrived to compromise it on the following terms.—He first made his *amande honorable*; then begged pardon in the public prints, and gave five hundred pounds to be disposed of in such charitable uses as the offended party thought proper. Some are of opinion, that to those engagements was added, a solemn promise of never going into Yorkshire again; but this we think apochryphal, and do by no means pledge ourselves for its authenticity; we must observe though, that from the unfortunate period alluded to, our Hero never visited the north, in which county he was considered, by the ladies, A SATYR: and by the gentlemen, who very laudably entertained a proper sense of female protection, A RUFFIAN.

THE cause of the young ladies nocturnal invasion could never be rightly accounted for. Beds were, no doubt, scarcely to be obtained by fair means, but it was yet extraordinary, possession should be obtained by means so unprecedented and extraordinary.

SCARCELY had our Hero recovered from the consternation, fatigues, and enormous expences of this business, when he was most disasterously involved in another, equally troublesome, and more humiliating. He, and the famous England, before mentioned, having some dispute respecting a debt, or the division of a play profit, became, from distinguished friends, the most inveterate, and avowed enemies. Whenever, and wherever, they had fair opportunities of calumniating each other, they were sure to indulge their reciprocal resentment, perhaps without strict adherence to truth. England, who was in the habits of turning every thing to his own advantage, at length determined to finish the matter to the Count's disgrace. He knew
of

of a party which was soon to dine at Medley's, in Round Court, and at which his quondum friend was to preside, and he was intimately acquainted with every other individual. One in particular who lay under pecuniary obligations to him, and was bound to his services, not only by gratitude, but fear, he justly conceived to be a proper instrument for his purpose. He engaged him to touch upon something in the course of the evening which should lead the Count to his usual abuse; and, then, affecting to be offended, to quit the room on a sudden, in apparent disgust.

ENGLAND, who critically adjudged the time, was stationed in the coffee room, below stairs, and of course enquired into the cause of his friends emotions. The matter being explained, in an affected Paroxism of sudden anger, he ran up stairs, and, without ceremony, or enquiring, flew at the poor Count, who, being extremely ill of the Gout, was totally incapable of defence, and loaded him with blows, reproaches, and execrations; and some others of the company interfering, met with the same fate. England was athletic, and resolute, and this being a *Coup de main* of his

Politics,

Politics, he spared neither strength nor agility on the occasion. The persons in the coffee room ran up stairs, and were witnesses of a scene not only ridiculous, but which actually established every intent of the devisor. Being at last prevailed upon to cease his coersion, England retired in all the puff of victory; but the Count was too much bruised and disconcerted, to be removed that night. He was therefore compelled to take a bed with his *merry friend* Jack *Medley*, and the next day, by advice of his Attorney, a law-suit was immediately commenced. Notwithstanding the Count's purse was open to every professional demand; notwithstanding the cause was assisted by the ablest council; notwithstanding the evidence was full and unquestionable; notwithstanding the assault was clearly established; and notwithstanding the presumed advantages of a special Jury; upon the issue of this important trial, which occupied the court of King's Bench for several hours; such was the complexion given to it by Lord Mansfield, that no more than ONE SHILLING damages was allowed.

When our readers recollect the several military transactions at Plymouth; the wonderful repulsive

repulsive efforts of *Fort Cloesinal* the summonses charges of the Count, when the Enemy were supposed to be on the point of landing. The last will and testament of the Colonel's bosom friend; the two conventions of the Mal-contented Officer; and, the applications to his Grace of Northumberland, they will not be surprized to hear, that, upon the death of Burbridge, the Colonel flatly refused to recommend the Count for the Majority, a promotion to which he had an undoubted right from service and seniority. He had, however, too high a spirit to be bar'd of this right by low and pitiful resentments; and therefore claimed, from justice and honour, what would, if possible, have been refused by illiberality and meaness. His attempt proved successful, and his commission, as a field Officer, was shortly made out, to the no small mortification of his enemies. The pre-eminence which he had heretofore derived from money, splendor, and spirit, was now established by rank; and, though it did not gain in proportion to the royal delegated favour, it yet lost nothing in the progressive dignity of his station. His field equipage,

and

and the ſtile of his table, did credit to his *promotion*, and his demeanour was ſuch as increaſed his reſpectability; and what is ſcarcely credible, that wonderful, intuitive faculty, which he inherited ſo ſtrongly from nature, enabled him to exercrſe the regiment ſeveral times before his Majeſty, and a number of General Officers, to their entire ſatisfaction, and, we may add, aſtoniſhment.

ABOUT this period, the health of Charlotte made it neceſſary for her to be frequently in London; ſeparated from a life of gay and giddy diſſipation, ſhe acquired a laſſitude and anxiety of mind and body, which all the variety of the country, and the ſtudd, could not remove. Chiddick, who had long been Phyſician to the *eſtabliſhment in King's place*, and retained as ſuch, with a fixt ſalary, ſtill ſupported his medical ability in her opinion, and to be near him, the Count indulged her with almoſt the ſole uſe of the houſe in Piccadilly. There ſhe amuſed herſelf with the decorations of fancy, and the ornaments of approved taſte; and, as her complaint was chiefly mental, there alſo, ſhe diverted thought by a variety of animated objects, ſeveral

domeſtic

domestic and foreign animals; but, above all, that wonderful parrot, whose rare and astonishing faculties, if it was not yet alive to prove their reality, would scarcely be believed, even by the most credulous. It was hatched in Bristol, and is perhaps as singular in its nativity as in its other qualities. It cost the fond Count fifty guineas, besides the expences of bringing to town, and we believe ourselves warranted, in declaring, that it would at this period produce five times that sum. Mr. Locke, in his inimitable discourse upon innate ideas, gives an account of a Peruvian bird, of this species, which he mentions as a wonderful instance of instinctive sagacity. It would, he says, not only repeat every thing it was commanded, but it would answer many questions which appeared to require a higher degree of perception. He states a few instances, and then concludes, with proving that *all* was derived from example. But when we compare the qualities of the bird in question, to those mentioned by the Philosopher, we must, without the imputation of partiality, give it the preference. *It* not only repeats all things, but answers almost every thing; and, so strong is its retention, that it sings a variety of tunes, with exquisite melody! it beats time with all the appearance of science, and, wonderful to relate, so accurate is its judgment, that if by chance (for it is merely so when it happens) it mistakes a note, it reverts to the bar where the mistake occurred, corrects it self, and, still beating regular time, goes through the whole with miraculous exactness. In addition to this we must add, that it sings whatever air is desired, and intimates an express knowledge of every request. To this aspiring imitator of reason, Charlotte devoted much of her time, and seemed to enjoy more satisfaction from its society than that of her own species.* But while she was thus striving to divert the symptoms of an hysteric affliction, and was almost become an established Convalescent, an accident happened at New-

* Such of our readers as were acquainted with the Count, during his military exploits last War, will perhaps discredit this account, because it will immediately occur to them that a Parrot, infinitely less sagacious, accompanied all his motions. The bird in question, was an acquisition long subsequent to the disembodiment of the Militia, and notwithstanding its great superiority, the Count, in gratitude to the first for services, nearly divided his favor between them.

market

market, threw her back exceedingly. Major O'Kelly's nephew, and heir, who was with her, as he muſt be with every perſon who knows his merits, a peculiar favourite, was gallopping over the Courſe upon a remarkably good horſe; the animal, by ſome unaccountable accident, fell, and broke its leg; young O'Kelly, was not materially injured; but as rumour ever increaſes in its journey, eſpecially when the object is misfortune, by the time this accident reached the ears of Charlotte, it was magnified to diſlocations, fractures, amputations, and all the melancholy conſequences, which might poſſibly have attended ſuch an event. At the intelligence ſhe expreſſed a kind of maternal grief, and it was many months before ſhe recovered from the effects. For this tender and ſincere affection, the Major always retained a lively ſenſe of gratitude, and often mentioned it with uncommon emotions of regard.

FORTUNE, which had for ſo many years, and with ſo much ſtability, favored our Hero, did not ſtop at the honor conferred upon him, in being appointed to the rank of Major. She had ſtill other gifts in ſtore; and the demiſe of the Lieutenant Colonel (Barlow) afforded an opportunity of augmenting her favour.

His old inveterate enemy, Chevaul, was still alive, and, as we may naturally suppose, still averse to his promotion. Of this the Count was well aware. To be applied to for a recommendation, was a thing of course, and Chevaul, if he was not sure of preventing his succession, was at least so, of shewing him his dislike by a peremptory refusal, as in the former instant. Judge, therefore, the mortification of this *Veteran*, when he found that, dispensing with formalities, the Major had applied to the Lord Lieutenant in person, and was actually appointed, without his suffrage, or knowledge to the second rank in the regiment. When mankind enter the shade of evening, every adverse incident disjoints the frame, the shadow lengthens as the substance fails, whether this, or the suits which Captain Hamilton, and the Lieutenant Colone brought, facilitated his dissolution, we can not determine, in imputing it to all, we believe we may not err.

Upon receiving his new commission, it was naturally expected, by those Officers who had ever been of his party, that the Count's elevation would be attended with some distinguished instance of friendship and esteem; but so far was he from expressing such sentiments, that to a splendid entertainment, of which Lord Derby and several of the Nobility and Gentry of Lancashire, were present, he did not invite an individual of the corps. A conduct so ungrateful, and so strongly tinged with upstart insolence, could not fail of producing great enmity and ridicule, and it is a fact, to the honour of those who was of that party, that even they joined in the general censure and disgust.

Notwithstanding this unexpected and unpopular decline of military favour, the importance of Colonel O'Kelly on the turf, seemed for a time, to increase daily. His opinion became more and more authoritative, and his company more and more solicited, in short he was regarded as the oracle of his profession. Our illustrious and all accomplished heir apparent was among the number

of

of those who admired his knowledge, and condescended to make a match with him in favour of the famous horse Rockingham, against the no less famous Duncannon, son to Eclipse, and O'Kelly's first favourite. The immediate bett was one thousand guineas, but, it is said, and universally admitted, that more than one hundred thousand were depending upon the event. The ease with which Duncannon won this important match, nearly involved him in the same misfortune which we have already noticed, when speaking of the *Manœuvre* practised upon Eclipse.

In a short period after this victory of Duncannon, the shameful parsimony of a close-fisted and narrow-minded Minister, gave the Prince of Wales a glorious occasion of displaying his heroic honesty. The facts are too well known, and the Prince's conduct too universally admired to need repetition, or applause. Among other expedients for the relief of his distressed tradesmen, the royal studd, though an object so alluring to a young and elevated mind, was cheerfully disposed of, and, with the other sacrifices to ministerial penury, Rockingham, the favourite of his
Royal

Royal owner, was knocked down by the hammer of Tatterfal, for a sum very far inadequate to his worth. Bullock, who, with Colonel O'Kelly, always appeared in the van of horse racing, made the purchase, and in some time afterwards challenged him to a second trial of Duncannon's speed. The invitation was accepted, and a day accordingly appointed for the contest. Betts were equal to the former, and the ground as much thronged; when, lo! to the disappointment and indignation of every one present, and the disapprobation of all who heard of the transaction, at the moment when the start was expected, the Colonel arrived; and, after looking for some time at Duncannon, who was then near the post, ordered him to be led off the Course. The confusion occasioned by this unexpected procedure can better be imagined than expressed; the Count was execrated in all quarters, and, it is thought, if he had not avoided danger, by a judicious retreat, he would have experienced the severest resentment of the multitude.

It is the common observation of judicious speculators, and observers of human nature, that

that dispositions alter with time, and that the different ages of life presents us in points of character extremely opposite. As our Hero advanced towards his '*Bourne*' he exhibited this truth in a variety of striking instances.

His brother, whom he had generously invited to see, and share his good fortune, felt its progressive force for many a tedious and painful hour, nor would even the gentleness and humility of his nature, repel the shafts of fraternal asperity. Often would he interrupt this useful, affectionate, and inoffensive kinsman with an unnatural moroseness, and when the persuasive eloquence of silence and submission pleaded most powerfully in his favor, such was the corrosive cruelty of age, that the breast which should have vibrated with the sympathy of blood, remained dead to every feeling but that of wanton resentment. His nephew, a young and ornamented character, and who he intended to perpetuate his name, did not escape the inconvenience of this incidental change. It is true, he granted him many gentleman-like pursuits; but, notwithstanding, few men ever launched into a wider sea of pleasure and disposition than did

the

the Count himself, so far was he from making any liberal allowances, that Andrew was always obliged to conceal the little indulgences incidental to youth. Caution, however, did not continually screen him: for, the old man would frequently lecture upon a mere suspicion of what his memory informed him, was inherent and unavoidable. Charlotte was the object least obnoxious to this increasing acrimony, and it is extremely probable that she least deserved it; the rest of his family were dependants upon his favour, but Charlotte claimed as a moral right, every indulgence in his power, and, we believe, she fully enjoyed her interest.

This alteration of temper, scarcely, however, exceeded the bounds of domestic concerns; our Hero still endeavoured to preserve the good opinion of the world:--his public munificence was supported without abatement, and his good humour, anecdote, and ease, still continued to make his company agreeable. His repartée and raillery too, were acceptable, though severe, and O'Rourke, whose soul was made of fire! could support his jokes with complacency. O'Kelly, who well knew, that, giving his name all the legendary consequence, ascribed to Hibernian anceſtry, it could by no means ſtand the teſt of competition with that of his friend and fellow Count, would yet endeavour to maintain precedency; and though that topic, of all other, was the moſt delicate, and indeed, dangerous with O'Rourke, the conteſt generally ended in favour of our Hero.

A SPIRITED part in, and a liberal donation to, the Hibernian charity, inſtituted in this kingdom, by the Earl of Bellamont, were the laſt public and praiſe-worthy acts of Colonel O'Kelly's life; at leaſt, the laſt we are acquainted with. The annual meeting of this charity, he attended as long as health would permit, and was once called to the chair by a reputable and benevolent aſſemblage of the moſt illuſtrious perſonages in both kingdoms. In which flattering ſituation, he expreſſed that propriety of conduct, which produced both approbation and eſteem.

THERE is another philoſophic remark, which, we believe, holds equally good, and ſeems to have been equally verified with that
already

already made. When we draw near the verge of another life, we grow folicitous, and reftlefs of our fituations in this. The Count now began to be weary, not only of his refidence at Clay-hill, but of the heterogeneous companionfhip which its proximity to Epfom, in a manner, compelled him to fupport. His old friends too, reminded him of old times, and he wifhed, perhaps, to avoid an unpleafing retrofpection. Be it as it may, about two years ago, he purchafed the houfe, domain, and eftate, called Cannons. which we are warranted in believing, was the firft Militia qualification he ever poffeffed. It muft be remembered that Clay-hill is in the county of Surry.

THAT expenfive and luxurious manfion, known by the denomination of Cannons, having, for fome time, been a topic of univerfal converfation, and in fact, a topic exceedingly worthy of univerfal communication, we fhall take leave to prefent our readers with a fhort fketch of its genuine hiftory. The late Duke of Chandos, while he enjoyed the lucrative poft of Mafter of the Ordnance, accumulated much wealth, and willing to leave

pofterity

posterity a splendid specimen of his magnificence and taste for architecture and improvement, made choice of a situation in the county of Middlesex on the Edgware Road, and about twelve miles from the metropolis.

WHAT made his Grace choose that spot, except it was to overcome difficulties, we cannot possibly imagine, for, in the formation of artificial ground alone, he expended many thousand pounds, to which the advantage of prospect was by no means adequate. The Mansion was superb and extensive, and the Out-offices, Gardens, and Grounds, elegant and beautiful. It was in fact, as has been mentioned in the daily prints, the boast and glory of its owner ! but, notwithstanding all its original grandure and apparent permanency, it was doomed to be the very sport of time and fortune. When the Duke sold off every thing, Hallet purchased it at a price, supposed at the time not to be half its value. But, when he carried his intentions into effect, pulled down the Mansion, and raised up the artificial ground,---incredible to relate ! the materials altogether sold for more money than the whole cost him. Not satisfied

fied with this uncommon advantage, he converted the two avenue lodges into convenient and elegant houses, one of which was afterwards occupied by Sir David Lindsey, and the other by a person of equal fortune. From this advantageous purchase it passed to O'Kelly, who, it is said, was, considering the rise of lands, nearly as fortunate. The house in which the Count lived was built upon the scite of the first Mansion, and is centered in the midst of every thing desirable; Garden and grounds beautifully disposed, and one of the finest Deer-Parks in England.

A SINCERE deference for our readers, as well as compassion for human frailty, induces us to pass over several subordinate traits in the life of this very singular character; such, as uninteresting Coffee-house anecdotes; attempts at wit; nocturnal broils; and, the indecent intrigues of public and private Brothels. A life so varigated as was that of Colonel O'Kelly, must have abounded with the common occurrences of such scenes; but we hold it highly improper that they should be presented to the general eye. They are fit only for the depraved contemplation of sensual

and

and diffipated minds, and are in our opinion more injurious to virtue and fociety in general, than even the example of practical immorality.

In the latter period of his life, O'Kelly took many occafions to exprefs a difapprobation of his younger days; and, his teftamentary conduct plainly proves the dread which he entertained of that courfe by which he was fortunate enough to accumulate wealth. His enemies, and perhaps no man in his line of life had fewer, would, if poffible, depreciate his character by falfe reprefentations of facts, and by the exercife and fertility of invention. The ftory of Mifs Swinbourne, of Yorkfhire, they exaggerate, by accufing him of getting into *her* apartment; but, the truth is as we have ftated, fhe by fome unlucky accident took poffeffion of *his*. Such however is, and has been, the character of this Lady, as to place her beyond the fhafts of calumny. It has alfo been injurioufly reported, that fome time after his arrival in London, he was married to a woman of fome fortune, and having obtained poffeffion of her money, deferted her; but, this we believe to be entirely the fabrication of malice. No part of his fubfequent

quent conduct having ever manifested a tendency to ingratitude or inhumanity. Of his courage also some have spoken with contempt, yet, if he was deficient in that generous and manly quality himself, it was wonderful indeed; for, no man ever admired it more in others; and he was once compelled, by the intemperance of a hot headed countryman, to risk his life in a Duel, in which he conducted himself with coolness and spirit. However the practice of duelling may be decried by refiners upon moral rectitude, it is, in our opinion, not only necessary to the support of honor, but of justice also. It is an appeal which transcends every positive institution, and scares the scoundrel more than any possible consequence of legal indignation. In the public field of National duty, the heroic spirit is stimulated by emolument, by rank, by universal approbation.----In the no less laudable support of private rectitude, the worst consequences are to be apprehended; yet, among men of honor, and we mean by that, men of *virtue*, it is, and ever will be regarded as the only means of restraining the most exquisite violations of society ;--so far in support of O'Kelly's courage.

BEING

Being completely established in the delightful residence of Cannons, the proprietor became more select in his company. He was visited by people of the first class of his own sex, and a few female friends, who were by no means exceptionable; and here he flattered himself with the hopes of spending a long and tranquil evening; but, alas! infirmity increased, and night fell on a sudden. The Gout, that fatal, that constant concomittant of luxury and hard living, now attacked him with determined violence, and at length forced him from the gay scenes of conviviality, to the irksome bed of Death. For some weeks before his dissolution, nature kindly indulged him with a Lethargy, and thus happily softening the painful rigors of his disorder, he expired with every evidence of bodily ease. Doctor Warren was his Physician, and as far as human skill would admit, aided in the composure of his exit. When he found nature began to fail, he collected a degree of fortitude, not common to men in his situation, and under the circumstances of his life. He made a judicious disposition of his property, by Will, and, in truth, as his career was a lesson of wonder, so was his death an example of imitation.

FINIS.

Lightning Source UK Ltd.
Milton Keynes UK
UKOW06f1847210914

238953UK00004B/105/P